Underground Cities

Exploring the Secrets Beneath Our Feet

Table of Contents

Chapter 1. Introduction

Immerse yourself in a world of mystery and intrigue with our Special Report: "Underground Cities: Exploring the Secrets Beneath Our Feet". This comprehensive tour-de-force is far more than just an exploration; it's an invitation to experience humanity's often overlooked triumphs and persisting enigmas concealed beneath the very ground we tread on. From the ancient subterranean passages of Çatalhöyük, Turkey, to the complex network of catacombs underneath modern-day Paris, this riveting report ushers you into a realm shrouded in history, resilience and marvel. Yet, no technical expertise or spelunking experience is needed; your curiosity and thirst for adventure will be your only guides. With beautifully rendered maps, stunning photographs, and captivating narratives, this special report promises a journey that engages the senses, challenges our perceptions of living spaces, and most importantly, prompts reevaluation of what we thought we knew about human ingenuity. Prepare yourself to delve deep and unmask the stories that the earth has quietly been safeguarding for centuries. The underground awaits! Secure your copy today, and let's start digging!

Chapter 2. Unearthing History: The Origins of Subterranean Settlements

The origins of subterranean architecture are as enigmatic as the intricate designs etched into the age-old walls of these undersurface habitats. From humble caves serving as the cradle of our predecessors, to cavernous constructions amassed over time, these dwellings are the physical embodiments of survival, resilience, and human curiosity.

2.1. The Cradle of Civilization: Caves

Our story starts where humanity itself arguably began - the humble cave. The evidence is etched deeply in paleolithic cave art, from Lascaux, France, where scenes of hunting were meticulously painted and preserved, to Altamira, Spain, boasting ancient cave outlines that stretch back to 35,000 BCE.

The caves offered our ancestors shelter from nature's elements and beasts, while their inner walls served as prehistoric canvases upon which humanity wrote its first records. But these were far from purpose-built. Humans were but guests in these natural formations, little adorning or altering their homes, merely sequestering themselves in the earth's earthen bosom for protection.

2.2. Emergence of Man-made Subterranean Structures

It was during the Neolithic Revolution around 10,000 BCE where the tides truly began to shift. With the adoption of agriculture, man stopped wandering and started building. Now, the creation of man-made subterranean structures came to existence due to a combination of diverse reasons - climate, defense, or cultural beliefs.

The Neolithic site of Çatalhöyük in Turkey stands as an argument favoring the aforementioned statements. While the surface-layer of the settlement reigned with communal activities, beneath them lay an intricate system of tunnels and chambers that served more practical needs. These included storage of produce and a cool retreat from the sweltering summer heat. A more profound reason resides in their burial practices, where the deceased were laid to rest in these underground chambers as a mark of respect, echoing a belief system woven intrinsically with the subterranean.

2.3. The Ancient Underground City: Underground Metropolises

Fast forward to the Bronze Age, the heyday of the first known underground city, Derinkuyu. This immense subterranean metropolis, located in modern-day Turkey, rendered itself virtually invisible from the surface, and served as a shelter to approximately 20,000 inhabitants.

Derinkuyu is a testament to meticulous planning and efficient use of subterranean space. There's not merely housing and storage facilities, but impressive amenities like wine and oil presses, stables, chapels, ventilation shafts, and even courtyards. Given the strategic partitioning of areas and facilities, it's evident that these spaces weren't merely chosen for survival, but for entire social hierarchies and a layered way of life to develop undeterred by threats on the surface.

2.4. Whispers of the Dead: Catacombs

Similarly steeped in history are the labyrinths of catacombs scattered beneath the streets of Rome and various other European cities. Born out of necessity due to overcrowding in cemeteries, these underground crypts offered more than a final resting place.

The catacombs became critical places of gathering for early Christians at a time when Rome, the then bustling heart of civilization, was an exceedingly hostile environment for them. These subterranean corridors, thus, became not only places of burial but symbols of resilience, sanctuaries for a clandestine community practicing their faith far from prying eyes above.

2.5. East Vs West: The Subterranean dichotomy

The appreciation for these underground spaces fluctuated considerably from East to West. While most Western cultures associated the subterranean with death and secrets, Eastern civilizations like China saw these spaces as harmonious sanctuaries that aligned perfectly with Feng Shui principles encouraging a symbiotic relationship with nature.

This duality ensures that our subterranean history remains more than just a chronicle of survival and adaptation; it's a vibrant tapestry of diverse cultural beliefs, expressive methods of community building, and the manifestation of advanced engineering principles.

In conclusion, these hallowed subterranean spaces have come far from their prehistoric roots. Beyond the tales of human survival, invention, and persistence, they serve as a looking glass into our collective past. They are our milestones, etched in stone, echoing the saga of civilization's evolution – a testament to our resolve and versatility, the silent and unseen anchors that bind our history together.

Chapter 3. Living Under the Stars: The Ancient Labyrinths of Cappadocia

Tucked away in the heart of Turkey, resting peacefully beneath the surreal, moon-like landscapes of what is now recognized as Cappadocia, lies a testament to human resilience and ingenuity that stands almost unparalleled in history. These are the troglodyte dwellings and complex underground networks that offer an immersive look into the lifestyles of ancient civilizations who made the unforgiving terrain their home. Merely a scratch on the surface reveals a well-preserved canvas of evidence, narrating survival tales and civilizations built, quite literally, under the stars.

3.1. From Formation to Habitation

The birth of these underground abodes can be traced back to three to four million years ago, when a series of volcanic eruptions blanketed the region in thick ash. The ash solidified over time into a soft and easily carvable substance known as tuff. This geologic blessing combined with ceaseless human innovation resulted in an extraordinary habitat.

Early settlers in Cappadocia recognized the malleability and insulation properties of tuff, foraying into the creation of intricate shelters. Swelling from mere units to villages and eventually to sprawling underground cities, these constructions presented unique solutions to the challenges posed by nature as well as invading forces.

3.2. Architecture of Survival

A venture into these subterranean cities reveals an impressive network of twisting tunnels, vent shafts, and chambers, demonstrating the ancients' in-depth understanding of architecture and city planning. We journey first to the city of Derinkuyu, excavated multiple levels deep, expressing an architectural intelligence that few could rival.

Researchers estimate that Derinkuyu, among the largest of the underground cities, could shelter thousands of inhabitants, along with their livestock and supplies, for extended periods. Storage rooms for wine and oil, bedrooms, kitchens, chapels, communal rooms, bathrooms, and even a missionary school with smaller rooms for education are embedded within its labyrinthine structure. The design is such that air shafts service every level, ensuring the circulation of fresh air, even at great depths.

3.3. The Underground Chapels: Echoes of Faith Below the Earth

No chronicle of Cappadocia's subterranean cities would be complete without an exploration of their art and faith. Numerous chapels were carved from the rock, demonstrating the religious devotion of the inhabitants. The wealth and grandiosity of wall frescoes found beneath the ground rival, if not exceed, those found in surface-level dwellings.

The Dark Church, as it is now called, had no external windows, protecting the frescoes inside from sunlight. The name partially derives from the limitation of natural light and the dark ambience reflected in its illustrations containing scenes of the life, death, and resurrection of Christ, suffering minimal damage over centuries owing to the lack of sunlight and climatic conservation provided by the subterranean environment.

3.4. Life Submerged: The Social Fabric

Subterranean existence could not have been easy, despite the layered defense and amenities. It demanded a communal spirit and interdependence among the occupants. To manage potential shortages, the ingenuity in designing these cities extended to the storage of food and water. A significant number of rooms were designated specifically for food storage, and grape crushing pits for winemaking have also been found. These extensive preparations were indicative of the long periods of time the inhabitants were prepared to stay underground.

3.5. Discovery and Modern Recognition: Unveiling the Hidden Cities

The unveiling of Cappadocia's underground cities in the modern era has been nothing short of an archaeological marvel. Serendipitously discovered in 1963 when a local resident knocked down a wall while renovating his home, Derinkuyu alone has twenty discovered levels, of which only eight are currently accessible to the public due to safety constraints.

In conclusion, the ancient subterranean cities of Cappadocia provide us with a snapshot of early civilizations' adaptability, resourcefulness and resilience. A testament to humanity's incessant drive for survival, these cities represent much more than historical habitations. They are a narrative of our collective desire for preserving life and culture, playing host to centuries-old narratives and echoes of a time when communities thrived under the stars.

Today, they remind us of the depth and breadth of humanity's architectural and social ingenuity, standing tall as cultural and historical artifacts worthy of our deepest admiration and study.

Chapter 4. City of the Dead: Paris Catacombs and their Secret Inhabitants

If ever a city were synonymous with splendor and light, it would undoubtedly be Paris. Renowned for its romantic allure, intellectual vibrancy, and architectural majesty, the Paris that shines under the sun is duly celebrated. However, beneath this incandescent landscape lies another Paris, which patiently endures in the obscurity, silent and almost forgotten. Welcome to the Paris Catacombs- a realm that betrays a tale of dark grandeur, public health crises, fascination for the macabre, and an enduring symbol of the "City of the Dead".

4.1. The Emergence of the Catacombs

As you stand before the ossuary entrance, graced by the chilling epitaph 'Stop! Here lies the Empire of Death', a brief journey through time is requisite to ascertain why and how this subterranean city was born.

In the late 18th century, Paris faced a significant crisis. Its inner-city cemeteries, particularly Les Innocents, were brimming to such an extent that corpses often resurfaced, causing infection and disease. Consequently, the Council of State, headed by Louis XVI, decreed the extraction of remains from overflowing cemeteries and their internment in the long-obsolete Tombe-Issoire quarries under Montrouge. This project was assigned to Charles Axel Guillaumot in 1786, marking the birth of the Paris Catacombs.

4.2. Anatomy of the Catacombs

Strategic tunnels that had once supplied limestone for constructing Paris' monuments now hosted a somber spectacle of human remains. Evolving from an arbitrary repository to a carefully arranged ossuary, the Catacombs soon took on an eerie aesthetic.

The two-kilometer-long warren is a bewildering mix of narrow winding passages and walled rooms - repositories of bones neatly stacked, often with artistic and symbolic arrangements. At intervals, grave-markers are inscribed with profound musings upon mortality and the human condition. Venturing deeper into the labyrinth reveals tunnel walls lined with geological and architectural cross-sections, remnants of miners who once toiled here.

4.3. Uninvited Guests in the Empire of Death

The Catacombs aren't just an ossuary and a tourist attraction, they're also home to a subculture that dwells within their shadowy labyrinth.

Meet the cataphiles- a group of individuals who've made the Catacombs their retreat, defying legal curfew, and since the 1980s, have been conducting secret parties, film screenings, and concerts within these tombs. There are even tales of a makeshift cinema being discovered by bewildered police officers in 2004!

4.4. Guided by Shadows: Navigation and Exploration

Navigating through the labyrinth without a map is not advisable; one wrong step, and you could find yourself embarking on an unintended course, tailed by the sorrowful echoes of the past.

The Cataphiles, though, have over time developed a unique system of tunnels identification. These markings guide them through the maze-like structure, embodying a language that's inherently enchanting and shadowy. Often, their exploration is fueled by the thrill of discovery and the allure of the forbidden.

4.5. Preservation and Access

While the Catacombs hold a magnetic charm for thrill-seekers and history buffs alike, they also pose preservation challenges. In 2009, the Catacombs' intricate network was digitally mapped to hinder vandalism and unauthorized access, promising a balance between public curiosity and reverence for the deceased.

The limited stretch of legal access, which hosts around 500,000 visitors annually, offers enough to satiate the curious without endangering the ossuary. But that hasn't deterred rebels from continuing their furtive expeditions.

In the midst of the exhilarating darkness framed by countless skeletal remains, we glimpse Paris' seldom-told tales that remind us: every city possesses an underbelly, a secret, a darkness that paradoxically illuminates its history. Indeed, the Paris Catacombs, this City of the Dead, has its silent narratives and inhabitants etching poignant tales into its subterranean vignette, tirelessly, and seemingly unendingly. As your journey herein concludes, remember: we're merely brushing up against the bedrock of these underground stories. The Empire of Death still guards many mysteries beneath Paris's light-bathed facades. Just listen quietly, tread lightly, and maybe, just maybe, it'll whisper its secrets into your ear.

Welcome to the spectacular world beneath our feet. We're glad you joined us on this subterranean foray. Keeping this exploration of ours alive, let's dig deeper. Each discovery sheds more light on the darkness, and every new catacomb tells a story that's patiently waiting for discovery. In the next chapter, we're continuing our thrilling voyage beneath Melbourne, Australia. Until then, keep digging!

Chapter 5. The Hidden Haven: Edinburgh's Mysterious Underground

Beneath the fluttering Scottish banners and the haunting echoes of traditional Gaelic melodies, a stoic facade hides a labyrinth of historical treasures - the underground streets of Edinburgh. The surface of this Scottish capital city buzzes with life, while beneath, a complex network of tunnels and rooms tell a story vastly different from the apparent tranquility above.

5.1. The Beginnings

In the medieval times, Edinburgh was a small town, confined to what is now only the city center. Due to the scarcity of space and the natural shape of the ridge the city was built upon, the inhabitants decided to build upwards. Buildings reached up to 7 stories high with dark and dank closes running between them.

Where space was precious, ingenuity prevailed. With lack of enough land space, the solution presented itself as building underground, leading to a sprawling network of streets and houses. But these basements and cellars were not merely storage spaces; they evolved into an array of chambers, workshops, and residences intertwining in an intricate network beneath the thriving city above.

Edinburgh's underground city was a byproduct of an ambitious town planning decision made in the mid-18th century. The city fathers, in a bid to match the European style of architecture, proposed the construction of the now famous New Town which effectively buried the old city passing through the North Bridge, tucking it away in the soil of history, both metaphorically and literally.

5.2. The Life Underground

Edinburgh's inhabitants led a harsh and challenging life underground. The parallels between the city above, known for its enlightenment and intellectual thrum, and the city beneath, characterized by pestilence and poverty, are striking.

The underground had narrow corridors and small, dark rooms stacked one next to the other. A single room often accommodated up to ten people. The lack of sunlight, proper ventilation, and sanitation led to rampant diseases, making these hidden passages a breeding ground for epidemics.

Despite the hardships faced in living conditions, the underground city developed its own complete ecosystem. There were cobblers, blacksmiths, bakers, and even breweries operating from the depths.

5.3. The Hidden Tales

The mysterious underground city was not just living quarters; It had hidden chapels, vaults, secret tunnels, and a host of tales that run as deep as the city itself. Some streets like Mary King's Close, have tales of people being bricked alive during the outbreak of the plague, while others tell stories of illegal distilleries and smugglers.

Whispers of ghost sightings and eerie happenings have painted these ancient walkways with a layer of supernatural speculation. Echoes of the past, imprinted on the very stone, can be heard in the wind coursing through these narrow corridors, adding to the allure of this mysterious subterranean city.

5.4. The Rediscovery

Over the years, the entrances to this underground network were sealed off and the existence of this city was mostly forgotten, vanishing into the annals of urban legends. It was only in the late 1980s that an excavation brought the forgotten city back to light.

Efforts to map and restore these underground passages continue to this day. While much has been recovered, some areas still remain hidden from the public eye. History enthusiasts and thrill-seekers throng these passages, chasing the echoes of a bygone era etched in the veins of this subterranean secret.

Edinburgh's underground city is much more than just a relic of the past. It's a testament to the resilience and ingenuity of human life adapting to harrowing circumstances. Its tales of survival and adaptation continue to reverberate, whispering stories of a city that thrived, not just in the picturesque landscapes and the towering highlands, but also in the secret passages beneath the very feet of its citizens.

One cannot truly appreciate the rich tapestry of Edinburgh's history until they've descended into its cavernous depths, where history literally lies beneath their feet. Brave the eerie tales and venture underground to witness a fascinating chapter of the city that was - Edinburgh's mysterious underground.

Chapter 6. Life in Miniature: The Wieliczka Salt Mine

The laborious grind of pickaxes against rock surfaces, the monotone rhythm of miners digging in the dark, the musty air imbued with the sharp scent of halite—welcome to the intriguing realm of Wieliczka Salt Mine, one of Poland's national treasures and a testament of humanity's perseverance, ingenuity, and creativity. Here, each minuscule grain of salt whispers tales of a past filled with graft, faith, and artistic expression.

6.1. A Historical Voyage

Our journey into the depths of the Wieliczka Salt Mine commences amidst the backdrop of the 13th century when the first shafts were dug. The mine's fame spread quickly throughout the medieval landscape due to its wealth of 'white gold.' This seemingly infinite repository of salt became an economic lynchpin for the mighty Kingdom of Poland, etching its mark into the annals of national history.

During its golden era, salt was a prized commodity—more precious than gold. It was a vital ingredient for food preservation, an essential aspect of life in the pre-refrigeration era. Serving these early needs, Wieliczka played a vital role in strategic and economic prowess, with its operations at a scale unseen in the contemporary world—the mine was producing a staggering 8,000 tonnes of salt annually by the 16th century.

Centuries of mining chiseled an intricate network of tunnels, chambers, and lakes beneath the surface. Over 287 kilometers of passages sprawl out across nine levels, reaching depths of 327 meters—an astonishing subterranean city evolving layer by layer.

6.2. Life-Sized Art: Carved in Salt

More than just an industrial site, the Wieliczka Salt Mine transcends into the sphere of art and religion. The miners, staunchly devout, sought divine protection in their perilous work. They built chapels deep underground to conduct mass before venturing into the hazardous darkness or to offer prayers of thanks after a day safely concluded. Their devotion, expressed through their chisels and picks, can be seen in the numerous religious sculptures and bas-relief scenes carved directly into the rock salt walls.

These embellishments grew more lavish with time, peaking in the creation of the remarkable Chapel of St. Kinga. Here, everything from the floor to the embellished biblical scenes that adorn the walls has been carved out of salt. Even the dazzling chandeliers are made from dissolved and reconstituted rock salt to mimic the effect of crystal. Visitors often stare in awe at this enchanting exhibit of miner craftsmanship and devotion.

6.3. A Testament of Human Endeavor

The Wieliczka Salt Mine is more than an artistic sanctuary; it's also a testament to human endeavor and perseverance. Behind the impressive carvings and chapels lie stories of miners who risked their lives every day, descending into the darkness to persevere against physical strain, potential cave-ins, and the relentless threat of 'fire-damp'—explosive pockets of methane gas.

This was not work for the faint-hearted, but reverent determination, companionship, and an unwavering faith allowed them to endure. Constant threats forced the miners to innovate, leading to triumphs such as the deployment of water hydraulic systems, and the establishment of horse-driven treadmills for hauling up the salt—testaments to their ingenuity gracing the annals of mining history.

6.4. Wieliczka Today: From Extraction to Exhibition

The turn of the 20th century marked the beginning of the end for the mining operations. Salt prices on the global market were plummeting, and the vast labyrinthine complex was becoming increasingly difficult to maintain. By 1996, commercial salt mining was discontinued.

Yet, far from slipping into oblivion, the mine found a second life as one of Poland's most sought-after tourist sites—a role that it performs spectacularly. Today, nearly two million visitors a year walk its underground passages that showcase the union of labor, religion, and artistry. The mine also serves as a venue for concerts, conferences and even weddings in the stunning St. Kinga's Chapel.

6.5. A Subterranean Cornucopia

The journey through the Wieliczka Salt Mine, filled with dramatic stories, stunning sights, and testament to human spirit leads us to contemplate on a grander scale. This 'Underground City', echoes a microcosm of life above ground. Each crevice, each carving, each grain of salt is steeped in history, a contrast of painstaking labor and intricate beauty—a profound symbol of humanity's resilience and our timeless quest to shape the world around us, regardless of where that world might be. Wieliczka is indeed a life in miniature. It invites you to dig deeper, peer closer, and appreciate the tales woven by history beneath our very feet.

Chapter 7. Beneath the Land of the Rising Sun: Tokyo's G-Can Project

In the heart of Japan, nestled beneath the luminous glow of the metropolis, lies a marvel of modern engineering - the G-Can Project, Tokyo's extraordinary approach to disaster management against flooding.

As we begin this journey, imagine standing in a colossal tunnel shimmering with a turquoise shade evocative of the ocean's depth. You hear the echoing whispers of a concealed river coursing below, its rhythmic roar painting an awe-inspiring picture of the power cordoned beneath the city.

7.1. The Birth of the G-can Project

This monumental endeavor took root from a challenging past. Over the decades, Tokyo has been pummeled by a multitude of typhoons, inflicting massive destruction. The confluence of rapid urbanization, climate change, and geographical susceptibility led to mounting concerns about the city's flood management capabilities. In the wake of these issues, the G-can Project emerged as a forward-thinking solution.

This underground network tunnels, also known as the Metropolitan Area Outer Underground Discharge Channel (MAOUDC), was formulated as a proactive measure. Initiated in 1992 and brought to completion in 2006, the project represented a promising lifeline to protect the city and ensure its residents' safety.

7.2. Engineering Marvel to Withstand Natural Disasters

Erecting a structure of such magnitude beneath an active city is a testament to human ingenuity. Each of five silos measures 65 meters in height and 32 meters in diameter, linked by 6.4 km of tunnels located 50 meters below the surface. This gargantuan project required relocating 3.3 million cubic meters of soil, approximately the volume of three Great Pyramids of Giza!

The system is ingeniously designed to coordinate with existing waterways and canals, channeling excess rainwater to prevent flooding. Once fuller, the gigantic silos and tunnels come into play, dispersing the excess water and ensuring the serene flow of life above ground.

7.3. Technological Mastery Behind the G-Can

Intrinsic to the G-Can's operation are the massive 14,000 horsepower turbines, four of them, instrumental in pumping out water at an astronomical rate of two hundred tons per second. All of this is controlled by an advanced monitoring system that keeps a vigilant eye on rainfall and water levels, guiding the efficient working of the project.

The marvel doesn't stop at efficiently managing floods. The Japanese approach to sustainability is inscribed in their robust reuse policy, incorporating the excavated soil into various applications such as park landscaping and cement manufacturing.

7.4. The Human Endeavor and Ongoing Management

In these labyrinthine channels of the G-Can, we see a perfect blend of human will, scientific acumen, and the sheer power of technology. Thousands of engineers, construction workers, and planners risked their lives to give this massive project life, ensuring Tokyo's safety against nature's unleashed fury.

The management of this remarkable structure implies an equally impressive program. Regular patrols inspect for any damage or structural issues, ensuring that the G-Can remains operational and efficient. Training facilities at the location are also organized for emergency response teams, an element that adds to the holistic utility of this hidden city marvel.

7.5. The G-Can: More Than Just Infrastructure

With its speckled lights reflecting off the water and the colossal turbines humming steadily in the background, the G-Can takes on a surreal, almost extraterrestrial quality. It stands as a monument to the immense potential of human collaboration, exercising our most inventive instincts to ensure the betterment of society.

Despite its functional responsibility, the G-Can has gradually become a peculiarly attractive tourist destination. The stark contrast between the bustling life above ground and the hushed solemnity beneath it compels visitors to take a moment and marvel at mankind's capability of mirroring nature's wonders.

7.6. Extending the Legacy

While the G-Can project's journey is far from being a fairy-tale, it's indeed a testament of Tokyo's commitment to safeguard its citizens against the onslaught of nature. Moreover, it exemplifies a model that other cities can emulate, marking a trail for those battling similar challenges globally.

Thus, as we peel back the layers of Tokyo's underground secrets, the G-Can project stands as a bulwark of resilience and innovation beneath the Land of The Rising Sun. It embodies the fusion of human ambition, engineering prowess, and government initiative, illuminating new pathways in the realm of urban planning. Indeed, the G-Can forms an integral shard in the mosaic of humanity's triumphant narratives under the skin of our earth. It beckons us to reevaluate what lies beneath our feet and acknowledge the veritable cathedrals that exist out of sight but within the ambit of human achievement.

Chapter 8. Into the Abyss: The Moscow Metro During Cold War

The Moscow Metro, a pinnacle example of Soviet engineering prowess, conceals more than just miles of sprawling underground tracks burrowed into the bedrock of Russia's capital city. This gargantuan network of subterranean railways and stations, erected under Stalin's decree, stood as more than a milestone in urban development; it offered a functioning shield against the nightmares of the Cold War - primarily, the threat of nuclear warfare.

8.1. Operation and Design

The development of the Moscow Metro commenced during the '30s, in an era hallmarked by Stalinist architecture. The grandeur and intricacy of its early stations still affirm the intent behind their construction: to be a "People's Palace". Amidst striking murals, gilded mosaics, bronze statues, and ornate chandeliers, millions of Moscovites found their daily commute transformed into a display of state propaganda. The architectural grandeur was meant to evoke awe, pride, and a sense of belonging among the city's residents.

Yet, the design went beyond aesthetics. Each feature was meticulously planned to ensure the system's survival in nuclear fallout. The Metro's depth (in some places, over 200 feet below the surface), reinforced concrete walls, sealed entryways, and powerful ventilation systems were all designed to shield its occupants from the radioactive dust of a nuclear blast.

8.2. Dual Purpose Architecture

Though serving a dual-purpose as a civilian transport and bomb shelter, the Moscow underground managed to keep the latter detail largely concealed from the public eye. The behemoth system was designed with an aura of normalcy. Stations were outfitted with grand hallways and ornate chandeliers that intentionally veered the public's attention from their true purpose. Yet, strategically positioned within these cavernous stations were hermetically sealed steel doors, ready to transform the bustling hub into a protective shelter.

8.3. The Cold War and the Moscow Metro

In the height of the Cold War, paranoia and fear were the common denominators shared across East and West. The imminent threat of nuclear warfare provoked an urgent need for viable protective measures. The Moscow Metro emerged as a front-line defense against such apocalyptic threats.

Perhaps most recognised is the 1962 Cuban Missile Crisis, an event that brought the world to the brink of nuclear war. During the confrontation, the Soviet Union treated the Metro as an active shelter, readying hermetic doors and air filtration systems against the anticipated nuclear fallout. Ensconced underground, the Moscowites found an inadvertent sanctuary; tunnels transformed into makeshift dormitories, and platforms into community kitchens.

8.4. Legacy and Post-Cold War Developments

In the post-Cold War era, the Moscow Metro continues to bear the galvanising legacy of its dual-purpose design. Vestiges of its past as a Cold War shelter are still evident. In many stations, the hermetically sealed doors and insulations remain intact. Vintage air filtration systems, fallout posters, and Geiger counters stir up ghosts of the past.

Despite the passing of the Cold War era, the Moscow Metro's role as a possible bomb shelter has not completely evaporated. To this day, it retains its protective mechanisms — a grim reminder of the earth's not-so-distant nuclear tensions.

In closing, the Moscow Metro stands as a testament to human ingenuity and resilience in the face of potential annihilation. It represents a crossroads where the needs of the everyday intersect with the exceptional, conjuring an architectural marvel that has survived as a working testament to the past.

8.5. Featured Station Highlight: Kiyevskaya Station

\[

Station Name	Location	Notable Features
Kiyevskaya	At the Kiyevskaya Square	Its mosaics celebrate Russo-Ukrainian unity. It has direct escalator access to a bomb shelter.

]

Our peculiar exploration into the Moscow Metro provides vital insight into the social, historical, and architectural nuances of a city suspended under its own concrete shell. As intriguing as it is intimidating, the Metro roots us into the heart of Moscow's Cold War past — a past still echoing beneath the city streets, becoming increasingly harder to ignore as one ventures deeper into the abyss. Secure more of such journeys with our special report today and continue unearthing the mysteries that lie beneath our feet. Only then can we begin to fathom the depths of our history, etched into stone and shrouded in shadows.

Chapter 9. Underground Wonders of China: Longyou Caves and Dazu Rock Carvings

Immerse yourself in the east, to the sprawling and enigmatic land of China, where timeless marvels and ancient histories prevail. Embarking on this segment of our underground expedition, we traverse the mysterious Longyou Caves and delve into the awe-inspiring Dazu Rock Carvings. Prepare to be enthralled by tales of a clandestine world that has thrived beneath China's bustling landscapes, whispering of an ancient civilization and its otherworldly conceptions.

9.1. Longyou Caves: An Enigma Carved in Stone

Our first stop in the clandestine Eastern frontier beckons us to the village of Shiyan Beicun in Zhejiang province. Hiding beneath the serene ponds of this local setting are the Longyou Caves, an intricate network of caverns that were discovered as recently as 1992.

These caves defy conventional wisdom. At first glance, they appear as mere grottoes. Yet, the decades of exploration and research that followed their discovery unveiled that their origins are anything but ordinary. The caves were intrically hand-carved at a staggering depth of more than 30 meters beneath the Earth's surface, comprising of pools, rooms, gutters, and bridges. Unfathomably, despite their ancient origins, these subterranean structures exhibit exceptional architectural integrity.

The enigma lies in their construction. It remains an unsolved mystery as to how the people of antiquity, devoid of modern engineering and tools, meticulously carved these caves out of siltstone. Theories abound, yet certainty eludes. The lack of historical records and inscriptions keeps us speculating about the purpose and the people behind these monumental works of art in stone.

9.2. Construction and Architecture of Longyou Caves

Studies show that the creation of the Longyou Caves must have required the removal of almost a million cubic meters of rock. Considering the tools and technologies available during their speculated timeframe of creation (in the Qin Dynasty, around 200 BCE), the feat seems almost impossible. Yet, the caves stand in quiet testament to the perseverance and ingenuity of their creators.

Each cave is colossal, with an average floor area of a thousand square meters. The walls, ceilings, and pillars exhibit intricate and uniform chisel marks, hinting at a level of precision that, even by today's standards, would demand immense planning, coordination, and architectural prowess. Notably, these marks, in their uniform pattern and size, challenge the premise of them being produced by primitive tools.

Each cavern is equipped with its gutter neatly, designed to drain any inflowing water into the central pool. The gutters were carved slightly sloping towards the pool, an engineering strategy that enabled self-drainage, ensuring that the caverns remained dry. From the unwavering symmetry of the supporting pillars to the precise angles of the drainage systems, it is clear that the Longyou Caves are the result of sophisticated engineering and intricate artistry.

9.3. Dazu Rock Carvings: A Chronicle Etched in Stone

Journeying onwards from the mysteries of Longyou, we find ourselves in Dazu county, home to the renowned rock carvings of the same name. Nestled in the hills of southwestern China, these exquisite carvings elevate our understanding of the religious and cultural elevation of the societies of yore.

Dating back to as early as the 7th century CE, the Dazu Rock Carvings represent a unique confluence of Buddhism, Taoism, and Confucianism. They're an immaculate fusion of sculpture, calligraphy, and painting, rendering a cohesive narrative on moral, religious, and philosophical ideas prevalent in that era.

9.4. Marvels of Dazu Rock Carvings

Spread across roughly 70 protected sites, the Dazu Rock Carvings encompass an estimated 50,000 figures. The expanse and scope of these carvings are truly remarkable, with the most impressive located in Beishan and Baodingshan.

The Beishan site showcases the oldest carvings, most depicting Buddhist stories. Most notable is a carving popularly known as the "Weeping Buddha." The emotional depth captured in stone with this work, where the Buddha is portrayed weeping at the suffering of the world, is profoundly stirring.

A visit to Baodingshan offers a glimpse into the later life of Buddhism in China. Of particular interest is the Great Buddha Bend, featuring the Wheel of Life, a grand depiction of the Buddhist concept of Samsara, the cycle of rebirth.

9.5. Preserving Heritage and History

The Longyou Caves and Dazu Rock Carvings stand as a testament to the unmatched craftsmanship and ingenuity of ancient Chinese culture. Our exploration serves as a stark reminder of how many secrets lie hidden beneath our feet, waiting for us to discover, ponder, and appreciate. As we yearn to unravel these mysteries further, we also acknowledge our role as custodians of this hidden heritage, ensuring these centuries-old enigmas are preserved for future generations.

Inside the Longyou Caves, each stone tells a tale of indefatigable will and unparalleled vision, while in Dazu, each carving challenges us with its philosophical depth and relentless complexity. The sacred union of human effort and geologic canvas in these marvels heralds our ongoing journey into the heart of Earth's secret wonders.

Chapter 10. The Unseen USA: Seattle's Underground City and Las Vegas Tunnels

Our journey delves beneath one of the vibrant cosmopolitan hubs of the United States - Seattle, Washington - to navigate a city forgotten by many yet markedly influential in the region's history. We then transition to the arid desert warmth of Las Vegas, Nevada, where a labyrinthine network of tunnels hosts a less acknowledged but inherently human undercurrent.

10.1. The Founding of Seattle's Underground City

Traces of the underground city of Seattle date back to the Great Seattle Fire in 1889, which obliterated 31 city blocks. Rather than razing the remnants to the ground, dedicated settlers transformed calamity into opportunity. They raised street levels, transforming previously ground-level storefronts and homes into basements or semi-basements, leaving an echo of the past city underneath the streets of modern-day Seattle.

10.2. The Architecture: More than Hollow Catacombs

Seattle's subterranean realm is far removed from a stereotypical, eerie labyrinth of dark tunnels, void of life and color. The preserved architecture stands as a testament to a forgotten era, echoing rich narratives from the past with each arch, pillar, and stone-framed doorway.

You'll find boardwalks of lumber, sawdust-strewn floors, and traces of ornamental plasterwork, providing glimpses of once thriving businesses. These were the arteries and veins of Seattle, the marketplaces, and connecting passages where life was once abundant.

10.3. Urban Myth or Local Legend?

Mysteries shroud the underground city. Some say that the Seattle Underground was a haven for illicit activities, with long-forgotten bootlegged routes and speakeasies echoing the whispers of the Prohibition era. As we peel back the layers of speculation, we delve into surprising and captivating tales that add another layer of intrigue to this concealed metropolis.

10.4. From Past to Present: Walking Tours

The Seattle Underground is not simply confined to the pages of history books or kept as antiquated urban lore, but it remains a tangible and accessible element of the city's fabric. Walking tours of the Pioneer Square district, for instance, offer an immersive experience for the curious urban explorer.

10.5. Transition: From Seattle to Las Vegas

From the damp and historical bulwarks of Seattle, our journey takes us to a vastly contrasting landscape, the hot and dry desert city of Las Vegas, Nevada. While Las Vegas is renowned for its flashy casinos and unrestrained extravaganza on the ground, few realize that another unpredictable city lies beneath - a network of flood channels that are home to an unusual community.

10.6. Las Vegas Tunnel Dwellers: A Hidden Community

Deep beneath the glitzy facades of Las Vegas's renowned casinos, around 300 miles of flood tunnels crisscross the city's underground. Often overshadowed by the city's bustling surface life, these tunnels serve as a not-so-familiar home for thousands of the city's homeless residents.

10.7. Survival and Society in the Tunnels

Living conditions in the tunnels are far from ideal. Residents risk everything from hypothermia in winter to deadly flash floods. Over time, this subculture has developed its unique set of rules and orderliness, forming a semblance of underground society.

10.8. Tunnel Art: Voices from the Underground

Like the graffiti adorning urban structures, the tunnel walls of Las Vegas serve as an expressive canvas for the dwellers. Through art and personal messages, the tunnel residents share their experiences, desires, and hopes, creating a diary etched in darkness.

10.9. An Initiative for Change: Shine a Light

Initiatives like 'Shine a Light' are working towards changing the lives of the tunnel residents. Such stories remind us that the underground is teeming with humanity, resilience, and an undeniable desire for better, just as it is in the world above.

As we conclude our exploration of these U.S. underground realms, we realize that they are not just hollow tunnels or forgotten architectural ghosts. These hideaways blur the lines between present and past, between surface spectacle and concealed struggle, prompting profound new perceptions about 'living spaces.'

The unseen, buried under the dust of ages; resides not in abandoned ruins, but in the pulse of daily lives. They are infrastructure and home, history, and future, persistence, and survival, art, and stories. The part of our journey here ends, encouraging you to think, explore, and understand the human-life that burgeons even beneath the overt narrative that is often told.

The world continues to bustle topside, while the tunnels echo with tales of their own; two sides of the coin, set on the same landscape, etching stories simultaneously. Unearthing the quintessential sense of existence, thus, remains an open challenge, inviting discovery, empathy, and respect for the endurance of the human spirit. In the realm underfoot, a mirror is held to our conceptions and misconceptions about societal norms. Venture into the darkness with an open mind, for the stories that lie beneath are as vital and vibrant as those found above ground. The underground awaits.

Chapter 11. The Future Underground: Modern-Day Subterranea and What Lies Ahead

The world as we know it is largely seen from the surface; yet, among the fascinating perspectives that are often overlooked is an exploration into the mysterious world lurking beneath our feet. This chapter will take you on a journey into the depths of our planet, exploring modern underground architectures, cities and potentially, the direction our future urban developments might take.

11.1. The Dawn of Subterranea

Our exploration begins in the recent past, delving beneath busy streets and skyscrapers into the spaces of utility that have been quietly expanding in the shadow of our surface progress. As urban societies continue to grow, the surface has seen burgeoning congestion, prompting a novel look towards the availability of space underground. Thus, began the creation of extensive sewage systems, sprawling metro systems and utility tunnels, which have become essential to modern living. In many ways, these subterranean passages echo the vehemence of human progress, showcasing our resourcefulness, adaptability, and monumental engineering capabilities.

11.2. Beyond Utility: Dwelling and Commerce Underground

It's not just our essential services that disappear beneath the sidewalk – in various parts of the world, entire businesses and living spaces are being tucked away beneath the surface.

In Helsinki, the government has adopted a comprehensive underground master plan, which outlines the sustainable utilization of underground spaces for a multifaceted urban life. Shopping malls, swimming pools, and even churches find their place in Helsinki's bold subterranean blueprints. Fascinatingly, the city employs the solid bedrock beneath it for eco-friendly solutions such as heat storage.

Similar scenarios can be observed in Japan, where the constraint of space has birthed stunning underground shopping facilities like the Tokyo's Toshimaen Niwa-No-Yu and the Yamato No Yu, both luxurious retreats complete with spa facilities, dining spaces and overnight lodging.

Paris and Montreal, too, have implemented extensive underground malls, and are testament to our growing fondness for an existence mildly detached from the surface chaos.

11.3. Underground Cities of the Present

More audacious still are the tastes for entire cities nested in the belly of the earth. Setenil de las Bodegas of Spain and the underground city of Derinkuyu in Turkey are just two examples of subterranean cities where the majority of life is lived beneath the surface, insulated from the harshness of weather and the woes of surface congestion.

More recently, China has begun exploring the potency of subterranean real estate with plans to develop an "earthscraper", an inverted, 19-storey skyscraper buried beneath the ground.

11.4. Sustainability and Ecology: The Underground Advantage

Increasingly, architects and urban planners are considering the potential of subterranean development as a solution to numerous environmental issues. High-density urban living often comes with issues of heat island effect and overconsumption of energy for cooling and heating. Underground structures offer natural insulation, helping to moderate temperatures and reducing the energy demands of climate control.

Further, moving large portions of our infrastructure underground frees up surface spaces, allowing for the return of green spaces that can increase biodiversity, reduce air pollution and enhance the overall mental well-being of the population.

11.5. The Challenges Ahead

However, embracing a future underground is not without its myriad challenges. Regulatory frameworks often don't account for developments beneath the surface, and questions of property rights and safety protocols are not easy to answer.

Prospective underground dwellers are also confronted with the lingering human preference for natural light and open spaces. Overcoming this psychological hurdle requires innovative design solutions that can mimic the surface environment or provide satisfactory alternatives.

There are also substantial construction and ventilation costs, earthquake risks, and the possible impact on groundwater systems to consider.

11.6. Looking Forward: What Lies Beneath?

A future underground, while potentially a solution to overcrowding and sustainability issues, is a tantalizing unknown. As we speculate on the shape of cities to come, as we drill down and burrow, planning for transport and dwelling, commerce and leisure, we are venturing into largely uncharted territory.

Nevertheless, in spite of the challenges, it is an exploration that could well prove integral to our urban future. With patience, caution, and inventive design, humankind may yet herald a new age where cities beneath our feet become as familiar and essential as those that scrape the sky.

As we move forward, the success of these ventures will largely lie in how well we can balance our technological capabilities, our ecological responsibilities, and our collective vision for a sustainable, interconnected world.

In the grand scheme of human civilization, an era of modern-day subterranea could be just another phase of our constant evolution as we journey into the future. So as we begin to look inwards and downwards, we might just discover that the secrets, the solutions, and our future might well be beneath us, waiting to be un-earthed.